THROUGH IT ALL, I REMAIN OPTIMISTIC

Christopher A. Lavizzo

Order this book online at www.trafford.com
or email orders@trafford.com

Most Trafford titles are also available at major online book retailers.

Printed in the United States of America.

ISBN: 978-1-4907-3753-9 (sc)
ISBN: 978-1-4907-3754-6 (hc)
ISBN: 978-1-4907-3752-2 (e)

Library of Congress Control Number: 2014909544

Trafford rev. 05/22/2014

 www.trafford.com

North America & international
toll-free: 1 888 232 4444 (USA & Canada)
fax: 812 355 4082

CHAPTER 1

Death is Inevitable

MY EARLIEST MEMORY OF DEATH came when I was about 5 years old. I recall waking up on a Sunday morning to find out my maternal great-grandmother had a stroke overnight and was rushed to the hospital. I was stunned. There was a feeling of despair in the air as breakfast did not seem right. It was only me and my older siblings at home that morning as my parents and grandmother went to her side. She was my mother's grandmother and had been my primary care provider. The epitome of old-school, she made sure my knees and elbows were scrubbed with powder cleanser during my baths. She chased me around as a toddler with a bottle of Cold Liver Oil and a teaspoon. I hated that stuff. I can still remember the smell of it. She sang songs with me as we watched Sesame Street and Bozo on television. She was always there for me as a child, but now she was gone and I would never see her again. I felt so lonely and helpless. I don't remember crying for some reason. I carry the scar of her death with me always even as an adult. I can honestly say I have issues of abandonment with certainty to this day. Being the youngest of five children, I've always been used to the idea of having family around me. Our household was like that. It will show up as a sign of weakness for me in my adulthood.

My next touch with death came as a 5th grader. My best friend at the time had a sickly mother who was suffering from cancer. He had three older siblings who were just about the same age as my four older siblings. They lived on our block and he and I attended the same private grade school. His mom always seemed to be in her robe or was at the hospital. Her being sick had to weigh heavily on the family as his dad seemed to drink a little bit more as time wore on. He had become so miserable that he could hardly hang on. Once she passed away, they seemed to have that same dark cloud of despair over their home be lifted. My friend was either taken out of our school in the middle of the school year or the family waited until the end of the school year to move. The only thing I could do was be there for my friend to help take his mind off things. We watched a lot of "Three Stooges" and "Little Rascals" on television. We laughed at everything as most pre-puberty males would at that age and listened to anything made by the Jacksons as he was a huge Michael Jackson fan. I felt his loneliness and sadness as the family did their best to keep things as normal as possible for him. I think about them all the time and what they must have went through. They seemed to flow in unison as a family unit. Everyone had a role to keep things moving along. Their very survival seemed to depend on it.

The feeling of emptiness comes with death. It hits close to home and touches your heart in ways that are hard to explain. Everyone has and will experience death in their lifetime. It's inevitable. It's how you are able to deal with it that will define you and your character. Some people are defined by a death in the immediate family. It will either leave an unhealed scar or it will have no real effect. I lost an aunt to breast cancer, my first time hearing about the phrase "breast cancer," when I was about thirteen years old. She was always a breath of fresh air whenever she visited our home. She was loud, funny and very caring. She doled out hugs like candy to my siblings and me. She was very close to my mother as they gossiped all the time about whatever topic. Our household always seemed a little more fun, a little livelier when she was around. I miss her and yet I marvel at the man her son, my cousin has become. Seven years my senior, he is the married father of two beautiful daughters who would have made my aunt so proud. I know he thinks of her all the time. She was such a beautiful person.

The next time I experienced being around a family illness came as I was in my sophomore year of high school. One of my best friends in the neighborhood had a mother who was suffering from cancer. Wow. Lightning strikes again. She was the most beautiful, caring, loving mother out of all of my friends. She had red hair, freckles and was light-skinned. She was a great lady. She always wanted to make sure her only child was watched over as she battled for her life. I, along with all of the guys in the neighborhood kept a watchful eye on my little big brother. We looked very similar, but he was a couple of years younger and about 4 inches taller than me and about 40 lbs. heavier. I kept him by my side up until I was about 18 or 19 years old. We played a lot of sports in the neighborhood; strikeout (baseball) at the local grade school, football (tackle, no equipment) and basketball at the local parks. We also had our share of girlfriends as we were like wolves seeking out mates. We were something else as we had another friend from the neighborhood join us in our boyhood pursuits. His father had moved the family while the mother was still battling the disease. I tried to make it a point to visit and make the thirty minute drive out to see them from time to time. They moved to an area where I now reside, ironically.

I later reconnected with my "little brother" to find out that his mom had passed away when I was in my early twenties. Man. I cried my eyes out and that empty feeling had overcome me so much that I could hardly get over it. She was like a mother to me and I was so hurt that I was not around to say good-bye or be there for my little brother. Time had forced me to live a life that did not include my old friend. Life is like that, it keeps moving along. He is the proud father of three kids and is still my little brother.

I've often thought about my other friend's mom, my great-grandmother, my aunt, both of my grandmothers and my paternal grandfather and many other family members who all had died in my lifetime. It hurts and I miss them all so much. To me, they were all great people who made my world a better place to be in. All I can think of is the happy times we shared. I cannot recall any bad times for some reason. They will be forever a part of my life. All I can do to keep their memory alive is to tell my son and daughters about these great people who were a part of my life. I'd like to think that I made them all proud of me in some way. Having their approval is important to me.

CHAPTER 2

Boy to Man

SELF-DENIAL IS A BITCH.

I had no idea that I could be wrong about this, not me! But as time moved closer to the inevitable, it was too late. She was going to die and there was nothing I could do to stop it from happening. It was 1996 and Debbie was slowly slipping away from me. She knew it and accepted it. We had been married the year before and together since 1989. Our wedding was the perfect day, joined by many friends, co-workers, family and old classmates. Never in my mind was I to think what was going to happen a year later. I was too engrossed into our everyday life of taking care of our kids, going to work, cooking, cleaning and administering her shots. I am very sure she thought about it all the time as any cancer patient does. Your mortality is on the line and it is out of your hands. Her oncologist had just suggested that morning that hospice was inevitable, but I was too blind and hardly accepting of this fate. I was always the optimistic one in our relationship as that was expected from someone six years her junior. I had a knack for keeping things light and not so serious in our marriage. She was the more serious one, having been married before. She accepted her fate with grace and a passivity that I would later learn about.

But this day will always be with me for the rest of my life as it marked the end of us as well as the beginning of the next chapter of my life. I wasn't ready yet. "Baby, it's alright, I am here," I told her as she began to slip into what can be described as being incoherent and not fully making any sense when she talked. She was fidgety and uncomfortable that night. I held her tightly, rocking back in forth. "I love you," I told her. "I love you too," she said back to me. Those were her last words. She stopped breathing. I could not even breathe. I could not scream and cry, for the kids were asleep in their room. I was numb. I tried to administer CPR, but it was pointless. All I could do was call for help. The paramedics arrived soon but by then I was pretty useless to them. She was already gone. They whisked her away to the nearest hospital but I knew it was too late. That scene will be with me for the rest of my life. My eyes tear up just thinking about it. It was my pain and my pain alone to deal with for the rest of my life.

Self denial is a bitch.

In a controlled-panic, I contacted all of the family and friends I could think of; her former boss, who was a federal magistrate, her mom and dad, her sisters and my parents. All of the responses were the same, silence, followed by pain, sorrow and regret. I kept the calls to the point and short, for I had to hurry to the hospital for the final act. I left the children asleep, totally oblivious to what transpired a mere fifteen minutes earlier and headed to the emergency room to identify the body and make funeral arrangements. I was twenty-nine years old making decisions on the spot as if I were in my sixties or seventies. Having family by my side would be slightly comforting if nothing else for me. I was crumbling away on the inside. I was growing up in a matter of minutes.

Having gone back to our apartment, I was met up with family members who did not want my kids to be there by themselves. Her two sisters and their family joined by my oldest brother. It was as air of despair in the place. But we were all glad to be around each other. We comforted each other. My oldest child, then my step-son awoke to all the whispers and movements in our home. "Alex, we are so sorry. Mommy's dead." He was told. "It's ok, as long as I have Bubba (the name he called me, the very first word I taught him as a toddler), I'll be ok." Wow, words coming from a seven year old at a time of despair. My first-born was two years old at the time and she cried and longed for her mother. I held her in my arms tightly and told her that everything was going to be alright. My family unit was reduced to three. In a span of six months in 1996, I lost the Catholic leader of Chicago, my paternal grandmother and now my wife. It was a very painful time for me. I lost all faith in God at that time. How could this happen to me? I was never going to be the same. My parents stayed with me the longest time after her death. They knew I needed them to be there. The kids became my salvation.

I always hated the thought of being labelled a widower, but that is exactly what I became. There was more to me, I always thought. But that was what other people thought of me during this time. It was easy to identify me as such. Family, co-workers and friends all did their part of trying to comfort me, but there was no real comfort I could actually feel. After taking some time off, I returned to work desperately looking for normalcy. I was numb for years after Debbie's death. Playing golf, pick-up basketball and playing 16" softball just became temporary fillers to occupy my empty time and loneliness. I kept busy for the sake of being busy, no rhyme or reason to it. I craved to be around people for some reason. Hearing another voice was soothing to me.

I also became the most available bachelor at work as I was looked at in an entirely different manner. I had become the office gossip again as that's where Debbie and I had met. Romantically linked to every single female in the federal building became utter nonsense to me. Some of the gossip was comical, some true. Being so weak and lonely, I caved in to pressure, a regrettable moment in my life I wish I could take back. Loneliness became my weakness. I hated being this way. I let my guard down and allowed myself to be in some bad relationships I would not have been in in any other situation. I was easy prey. You live, you learn. I often wondered if I waited long enough to make myself available. I had no filter and was easily influenced because I was lonely. It's way too late now. Not everyone feels your pain and anguish, nor do they want to. There's a lot of selfishness out there.

All I had were my kids to keep me busy and work as I also had the daunting task of being placed in my late wife's work position as a courtroom deputy for a federal district court judge. Talk about taking one for the team . . . . Not sure why to this day I did my then-supervisors, that huge of a favor. It would later come back to haunt me as I was later replaced on a whim, without any explanation leaving me a very bitter and angry man on top of what I was dealing with as being a widower and single parent. The work was challenging and consistent. I worked constantly, weekends, evenings, you name it. I did all I could to satisfy my immediate boss, a U.S. District Court Judge. Her caseload was tremendous, due to the amount of cases dumped on her from other seasoned judges upon her confirmation as a federal court judge, but ultimately, despite helping making a dent and making her caseload manageable, I was removed and reassigned to another department within the courts. I wasn't given an explanation or thanks, just a word of caution to look out. I was being watched and was looked to be removed from the courts all together. I was pissed. What did I do that was so bad?

Government positions are like that, you can be reassigned within the same office, and your salary is guaranteed for up to two years. In that time, you should find replacement employment that fits your salary. Now, if the parameters of the position change and you find yourself all of a sudden "not qualified" for a position you previously held, well then you are up shit's creek as your salary can and will be comparable to the new position you are placed in. In other words, I was to be screwed for no other reason than a cost-cutting effort and the flexing of muscle by a new Clerk of Court. To hell with the 12+ years of service I held, out with the old, in with the new, cheaper version. I did not bow down to new management as my co-workers did. There was a surplus of employee movement going on during this time. I lost a lot of co-workers in the process. I was defiant and impassive as to what was actually going on. I was a great employee who moved up over the years, promotion after promotion. I was overconfident that I was untouchable, feeling my past accolades were sufficient.

Lucky for me, I had made many friends throughout my time in the courts. A federal magistrate that I knew needed a courtroom deputy since his clerk had applied and accepted a position with a federal judge. He sought me out and saved me from the department I was in. It was an upgrade for his clerk, which brought me some time and opportunity.

I was able to maintain my salary scale and work for a great man and not have to go through a formal application/interview process, which I am sure pissed off the "new powers that be." I clicked immediately as his clerk, doing whatever he needed for me to do. I was so grateful for the chance, so much so that when he found out he was not going to be retained and faced retirement a couple of years later, I turned down a position with another magistrate who had an opening, just to serve out my boss' last final days. I owed him that. Loyalty meant the world to me in a place that long forgotten what that meant. I was reassigned back to my original department, where I first was hired. I applied for a position I had just held as a new magistrate was assigned. He went with another person who was not as familiar with the cases he had just inherited. I even applied for a position as a swing clerk, only to be told I was not qualified even though I had completed the same duties before. Imagine that. The walls were closing in on me. Other available positions within other federal offices weren't paying as much as I had earned, so I was really desperate for new employment.

The place that was once my refuge had now become stifling and bothersome. I loathe every moment of entering that place. Deception, betrayal, lack of compassion and an overall feeling of lack of respect was the norm of what I perceived every day. It takes over your ability to do the job you were originally hired to do. All that I had achieved, all that I gave and sacrificed meant absolutely nothing to those I had worked for. It ate me up inside. I was slowly unravelling. I felt that my twelve plus years of service meant nothing to the powers that be. I was on my own and no one looked out for me anymore. New management was the new sheriff in town and I was a stranger in town. Add to the equation of being in bad relationships with certain co-workers and the death of my maternal grandmother really made life miserable for me. I went from new kid on the block, to the golden child, to the available widower, to the petulant child, to ex-employee in less than 13 years. I never thanked them for building me up and tearing me down. Maybe one day I will.

CHAPTER 3

Life Goes On

FTER LEAVING THE GOVERNMENT FOR greener pastures in 2002, I embarked on obtaining a real estate license at the advice of my mother who was doing the same in Las Vegas. I took the necessary classes while I still was at the federal courthouse. I passed the examination, and went with a very reputable real estate company. These were challenging and exciting times for me, as I had to make a name for myself as a sales associate and realtor. It was a stressful time as well, as everything depended on my ability to close deals and get my clients to closing. I had extensive training and was let loose like a puppy on a leash. That's the nature of a commission-based position. I worked six to seven days a week, sixty hours a week. I was sniffing out clients, left and right. Open Houses, Swing shift on phone calls, cold calls, you name it, I did it. I ultimately became the trusting liaison of these families. I was shaping their lives the best way I could. Any realtor will tell you that their success is solely based on their ability to obtain clients who were financially sound. Imagine that. If you want to earn a living and maintain stability, you have to court and side with your clients' FICO score, no matter how hard or how long you worked. That sucked. Feeling the pressure to make my yearly quota set by my broker manager, I looked for a second job that had some other benefits as well, to help ease my stress. I was chasing the money trying to maintain a modest middle-class lifestyle.

Paid vacation, health insurance and some sense of stability were important factors for me. I needed something that fit my background, my experience. I needed to also maintain my license as I felt I worked so hard to get myself to this point in my life. I found a position as a manager for a law firm. Perfect. They needed an overhaul of their filing system. I needed security. It was a natural fit. It was the second best job I ever had up to that point in my life. The work was methodical and easy. I managed high school students who became like nieces to me. My co-workers had become like family to me. We had our moments of laugher, mixed with hard work and an appreciation and respect for one another. I managed to balance practicing real estate in the evenings and weekends and oversee the law firms' file room Monday through Friday. Life was pretty good up to that point. I thought I could handle this job with ease, as I still was able to court clients who were looking for homes. The real estate market was still booming and thriving. And I was even managing the firm's co-ed softball team.

I had no idea going into real estate that I'd have the opportunity to meet and court professional local area athletes who needed property. I had hit gold by having such people on my rolodex. I could call on their family members on a whim as I had maintained their trust even after deals were done. I also was blessed to have met and courted couples who became like family to me. As long as they were serious about the process, I was there for them, no matter what. Loyalty is like that for me. Leaving was going to be hard for me. I never thought I'd be so lucky again.

Fast forward to 2006, I was having stomach pain, a feeling of constipation as well as some blood in my stool. I checked myself into the Emergency Room. My oldest child and my fiancée went with me and were very concerned. Tests showed that I had some issues. They sent my results to my doctor and told me to see him immediately. Unfazed, I followed directions not knowing what was to ensue. After a few days, I met with him and he ordered me to get a scope of my colon. That procedure was pretty quick and easy. No pain at all.

The results revealed that I had a tumor in my colon. Colorectal cancer. I was floored. I had no medical history, no real family history of cancer as my maternal grandmother had passed away from lung cancer due to her smoking habit, nothing that could explain this bombshell. How did this happen? Me? I was not a constant smoker. I had an occasional cigar whenever I golfed (two to three times a month). I was not a heavy drinker. Beer was my preference and generally consumed on social occasions. I had a fairly healthy lifestyle up to that point. No high blood pressure. Cholesterol was moderately high. I was a bit overweight due to lack of consistent physical activity. What was it? Oh my God, it was stress. It had to be. There was no other explanation. I had to make changes in my life as I felt I needed to get control of this thing. Keep it together, Chris. Keep it together. Ten years had passed since that night in December 1996, but I now I had to face another challenge that was forever going to define me.

The words you never want to hear from a doctor, "the mass we found is cancer." It was at that moment that I was frozen in disbelief. It was not the first time I heard those words from a physician but you never want to get used to hearing it. My emotions went from shock, the aforementioned disbelief, anger and focus in a matter of seconds. I am not sure what scared me more at that point, the memory of going through the whole gambit of cancer (as a widower of cancer and now as a patient) again or dealing with my own internal anger that can be quite nasty at times. Keeping my emotions in check was going to be my biggest test throughout this process. Through it all, I remained strangely optimistic even though all around me is chaos. My fiancée is sad and emotional, a trait she rarely shows. My kids, stunned. My parents were in disbelief. My focus has never been sharper for what I need to do. I can't help but think about Debbie and her struggles to deal with the treatments, I remain optimistic. Life is truly ironic that way. My life was going to depend on it.

Nonetheless, this was something I knew deep down inside my heart that I was going to face this alone, despite the self-control and confidence I displayed to everyone around me and despite the support I was getting from family. This was my battle and my battle alone. No one else is getting poked and prodded on. No one is dealing with the uncertainty of knowing what their future was going to be. No one else was going to be potentially losing these children, and them losing a father. What was also certain was that my mind was going to be moving at the speed of light worrying about my fiancée, my children, my parents, my family and all of the things I still had to accomplish in life. It was a tough position to be in despite my history with cancer as a spouse. For me, there was no family history of cancer to rely upon for wisdom and comfort. This was going to test every ounce of energy, will and confidence I had within me.

Life has its ironies. One day you're living the American dream of being married with kids, working and planning my future, the next day you are in the fight of your life. I was always an optimist at heart, looking for the brighter side to dark and dreary situations. This situation was going to be no different.

As a first-timer, I was pretty naïve about the process I would have to go through as a patient. I completely trusted my doctors and the care I received. I also did some research and found that since the cancer was caught early enough, I had a really good chance of beating it. It was very comforting and gave me some sense of confidence.

I was referred to an oncologist, whose office was across the street from my real estate office. Perfect. The good news was that the tumor had not spread to any other part of my body. Even better, there was a sense that I was going to be ok. Because ten years had passed since Debbie had passed away from breast cancer, there had been so many medical advances since then that it gave me comfort amid all of the anxiety of receiving this life-changing illness. The game plan for me was pretty simple; a round of chemotherapy, radiation, surgery to remove the tumor followed by another round of chemotherapy, all to be completed within a year. I could still work and pretty much function as if nothing was really wrong physically with me.

Mentally? That was another matter. My mind was on full blast all the time at this point. So many questions, so many thoughts kept me occupied. My life had been reduced to watching a nonstop video in my mind, looping and looping, over and over. Getting refocused was going to be harder than I thought. I had thoughts of family members who had passed away as angels looking over me. Work was going to be my solace again, but not too much of it. Faced with some tough decisions, I decided to walk away from my real estate career, as I felt the stress of chasing clients and getting them closing was the main culprit of this cancer.

Financially speaking, curtailing my business all the while of having fees and dues still hanging over my head was not a great idea or a great option at this time. Something had to give. I chose to walk away from the really good commissions and relationships with clients, which I really got used to having. Financially, I was going to be lost for a while, trying to reclaim what I thought I'd earned over the years. It was the chase for money and lost income I felt, that would be my undoing.

Obviously, I needed health insurance from the law firm to ensure my treatments were going to be covered. So leaving them was not an option. The chemotherapy was fairly mild and had no initial ill-effect on me. I was able to work full-time, receive treatments and sleep off the chemotherapy in my system over the weekends. We kept it simple. I wanted my children and wife to maintain their life and schedule as if nothing was wrong with me. That was important to me. I felt as though I had the flu for about two weekends out of the month. Physical weakness, no major hair loss except on my body was very tolerable. As fast as I was able to build my body up with good eating and walking to and from the train from work, which was about just about a mile, from Michigan Avenue to Wacker Drive, it got broken down with the chemotherapy as every cell in my body was slowly exterminated. It was going to be ok, I thought. Sleeping was going to be my therapy.

Being one of the youngest patients at my oncologist office was a bit unsettling at first. But I learned to stay focused and get through each treatment with resolve and a smile on my face to my nurses and technicians. Each session, each visit for radiation became such a routine that you get numb to the idea. In fact so, I stopped counting the sessions just so I would not be obsessed over them. This was best for me. I had about two weeks' worth of sessions of radiation. I was not scarred or burned on my skin. It was painless. I got so used to the idea of taking off my clothes in front of strangers that it was nothing for me anymore. I became a bit of an exhibitionist. I had to try to find humor in my despair.

CHAPTER 4

Illness Changes Everything

*T*HE NEXT THING I KNEW, I was being prepped for surgery. This was going to be the easy part, or so I thought. Being a surgical patient the second time around was a little terrifying. A few years earlier, I had surgery to remove my tonsils and adenoids because of my snoring issues. That was a walk in the park compared to what I was about to experience. I had so many concerns but I kept them to myself. I put on a brave face as I was joined by my fiancée, my mother, my biological father and my half-sister at my bedside. The thought of being asleep, darkness, made me unnerved. Around me, everyone is chit-chatting as if nothing was going to happen. Get it together Chris, get it together. As I waited for the surgeon, who took a long time as he was performing other surgeries, I was visited by my old college roommate in the pre-surgery staging area. Wow, didn't see that coming. We talked for a while. It was surreal to see him as I was not expecting visitors just before going under the knife. I needed that comfort.

Coming out of anesthesia was very strange. I could hear voices, see shadows but not make out faces. I was very agitated. I could feel some pain all over my body but couldn't quite pinpoint the source. I was given a handheld button that was attached to a container of morphine. This was going to be my best friend for the ensuing week. I made good progress over the next few days. I slept a lot. Visits and phone calls from family and friends made my stay at the hospital very tolerable. My primary doctor made rounds and gave me updates that reassured me that I could be discharged as planned. All I needed to do was walk around the hospital floor and I could go home. That was all I needed to hear. I walked like a new born deer with trembling legs but I got through it ok. Every step was painful, but tolerable. I was on my way home!

As the youngest child of my family growing up, it was just what I needed to help me, having my mother there to help me. I was going to take all of this attention like a six year old. After all, I am and will always be the baby of my family. My now wife at that time, was my fiancée as we had never got around to set a firm wedding date. In my mind, we had all the time we needed. No rush. Neither of us was going to go anywhere and leave one another. It was something that was a given our minds. Loyalty is like that for me. Well, life has a way of opening your eyes to other possibilities and realities and what can happen in an instant. My mother stayed for about a week and as soon as I showed signs of getting better, she caught a flight back home to Las Vegas.

My oldest child was preparing for prom as he was invited by a young lady who was a year older than him. As a father, I was very proud and happy to see him click with someone. She was a very attractive young lady who lived nearby the high school. I was not able to see him off at her home for pictures as I was still healing and had problems moving around with fresh stitches on my abdomen. I did manage to help him with his tuxedo as he hadn't worn one since he was six years old. My fiancée filled in for me as pictures were taken at the young lady's home. It was very nice from what I saw from the pictures. I felt so bad that I could not be there. My place was to be there, I couldn't help but think. He didn't seem to mind but as long as he had a good time, I was going to be ok about it.

One of the conflicts I was dealing with in my household off and on over the years was with my fiancée. She has a very different way of communicating and tends to be a bit abrasive in the way she handles routine communication matters. I have two kids from my previous marriage and one with her. My position has always been that I felt strongly that my two older kids and wife can benefit and learn from one another because they share a common trait not everyone has; losing a mother at a young age. There have been numerous times that I felt as though I have put my own happiness aside for all of their betterment. I would like for her and them to heal internally, communicate more effectively as well as learn to treat each other with some form of compassion, empathy and nurturing. Not too much to ask, right?

Admittedly, it's been and still is a work in progress. It's been stressful at times. She's had some counseling prior to our relationship but those appointments pretty much have ended. She's done some journaling and taken some prescriptions for mild depression (no longer) that is a direct result of her losing her mother when she was younger and not having much of a relationship with her father. It has defined who she is as a person. But, it's pretty tough and stressful to be the fixer and glue to this family when I feel as though I have so much working against me. Yes, it's worn on me over the years. Communication is poor because she never admits to any wrongdoing. Being the super-hero just doesn't mean as much to me anymore, with trying to "save people" who don't want it or need to be saved by me. The burden weighs too damn much and no one gives a damn about you, so why bother? It has been too burdensome to deal with. It cuts to the core of who I thought I was. I can't do it anymore when I am fighting a foe that is not willing to engage.

A few years earlier while I was still employed by the courts. I had been flirting with the idea of finding and reconnecting with my biological father. You see, my parents divorced when I was about 3 or 4 years old. I remember it quite well. Nevertheless, I had to come to terms with that I was not biologically a Lavizzo. It is my adoptive name from the man who married my mother and raised my siblings and me after "the incident." I cherish this name with all of my heart. I also knew that there was another truth out there I would have to face at some point in my life. The older generation never speaks about the past, especially when there is pain involved. I had to piece my life together, well after the fact. Oddly though, I am ok with it. I know who raised me, what it must have taken and the love involved. That is the glue that binds me, love. Loyalty is like that for me.

My fiancée recommended that I should write a letter to my father to reach out to him. Most of my life I knew where he lived, but I was always too scared to show up and say, "Hello, I am your son." Writing a letter seemed like a better option. So, I wrote a letter explaining who I was, what had happen to me and not to worry, I turned out pretty good. Mom did right by me. I also explained that I held no ill will towards him and that I am healed from all of the years that had passed. The letter bounced around his apartment complex because there was more than one Clifton Hill living there. Go figure. He wrote back, and after a while, we exchanged letters. He became a part of my life again. He was so relieved. My youngest child was born with red hair and fair skin. My mother clued me in on a visit to Las Vegas to let me know that my paternal grandmother had that trait. She had passed away suddenly when my father was a teenager. Her death affected him and his siblings in so many bad ways. He most certainly carried that scar his whole life. He carried an anger and bitterness his whole life. It defined him.

It was also during this time I also tried to see a therapist to help me sort out some things in my personal life. I was in a flux, always thinking I was unravelling and could not keep it together anymore, especially with work and Debbie's death. After a few sessions, I ended seeing the therapist because I had an "a ha" moment. Things clicked and I seemed to figure out my purpose again. I felt that things weren't so bad and that it was a part of life. I was dealing with chapters of my life.

I returned to my oncologist office for a follow-up and planned for the next round of chemotherapy. She explained to me that everything looked great. There was this new experimental chemotherapy that may be beneficial to me. I fit the profile of the test subjects. Oncologists are like that. They tell you your numbers are just about perfect and without batting an eyelash, want to give me more chemotherapy despite the surgeon saying he got all of the cancer during surgery. Really? Crap. I was in a flux. I gave it some thought. I got the opinions from family. Fine. I'll do it. I was a bit overconfident as I managed to get through this the first time around. I managed to get in about three sessions when I started losing feeling in my hands. Uh, oh. As soon as I mentioned this to my oncologist, she ended my treatments. This was going to be my introduction to Peripheral Neuropathy. Nerve damage. Numbness. Stiffness. Non-stop. Too late. Shit. Playing sports was never going to be the same. Side effects suck.

What had given me joy in my life was going to have to be replaced with something else. Your hands and feet are needed in just about everything you do as an athlete. Running and walking, catching, swinging, putting, shooting a jump shot, it all became something I was going to need to adapt to. Not easy. You do something for over thirty years then have to get used to another way of doing things was going to be another challenge. Even typing is now a chore that doesn't come easy any more. Pure joy for me is now over. Good thing for me my makeup was that of a competitor. That was going to make all the difference for me in these ensuing years.

The nurses and technicians gave me a wonderful send-off at my last chemotherapy treatment. I was considered in remission. Wow. I had no idea what to expect. They made me a poster board, signed by everyone in the office and decorated with balloons. They even had a cheer for me, complete with a high kick from the nurse. Really cool. I was stunned and really overjoyed.

There are times when I try to recognize the appropriate time and place to resolve conflicting issues in the appropriate manner. It is a work in progress as I feel as though I could improve on minimizing my penchant for being passive and non-confrontational in certain situations where it may be helpful to be assertive and competitive when dealing with conflicts. I internalize things. I try to measure my words and use them with purpose. I guess I could also balance a little less sarcasm and demonstrate a little more openness that allows those closer to me to be able to communicate with me in a way that makes them feel comfortable. It used to be that I did not mind having someone confide in me in whatever made them comfortable. It doesn't happen as often as it once had. Perhaps it's just a coincidence. It seems to me that strangers feel at ease and can open up to me. Those closest to me have a hard time completely opening up to me. Perhaps it's still there and I am just focused on my own issues with education, employment, health and marital. For these are issues of stress that are a major part of what I deal with on a daily basis in dealing with cancer. It's a bitch to deal with.

On Thanksgiving 2006, I am planning a feast at home. I do the majority of the cooking; turkey, macaroni and cheese, dressing, green beans, my fiancee does the rest. I make several attempts to contact my father to invite him. No answer. He was very old-fashioned, I had learned, and he had no answering machine, so I couldn't leave him a message. So I kept calling, no answer. Oh well, that is so like him, I think nothing of it. I get a call from my half-sister, the day after Thanksgiving telling me she got a call from the apartment complex where he lived, telling us to come down in a hurry. I can tell she is worried. My mind is racing the entire trip wondering what was wrong. I arrive there to find a decomposed body sprawled out on his bed. There is a smell of burnt coffee in the air. I know it is him because of the gym shoes I gave him are on this body. The hair on the head is completely white, yet again another sign. I am numb. My sister was near hysterics.

The police are there to investigate and were the ones who initiate the coffee smell. It was to take the smell of his dead body away. We notified family to let them know. The whole scene was surreal. There was no foul play and it was determined that he had a heart attack. He left work on Sunday complaining of not feeling well, we later found out from his manager. He made it home in time to clutch pictures of my half-sister and I as kids. We were on his mind up to his death. He laid on his back dead for five days before he was found. I stayed shocked for months. I was just getting to know the man who made me only to have him taken away. It hurt for a while but I am oddly ok about it. He would have wanted it this way. I am sure he knew he was dying, because he started mailing me some of his personal items. He collected things over the years and before I knew it, I was in possession of his cherished items. This is odd because I too, was a collector of comic books. I was definitely his son. May his soul rest in peace, I hope that he was at peace with how I turned out.

CHAPTER 5

Looking Ahead

*F*ALL 2010, AT THIS POINT of my life, I am a part-time student looking forward to finally completing my BA in Communications at Governors State University. My mind is totally focused on my studies with knowing I had a target date of graduation coming up that next summer. I decide to see my primary physician to have a simple check up, partially because I am having some groin area pain, due to moving a piano I had purchased from a neighbor at his estate sale. He was an older gentleman who was recently widowed so I realize that I need to put more push and pull for this task. The good news was that he lived right across the street from me. The bad news was that I pulled something and thought I may have a hernia, thus the trip to see my doctor.

Accompanied by my wife, during the examination, I mention to him that I may have pulled something and he was able to confirm my self-diagnosis. He feels around a little deeper with his examination of me and notices a rough area on the surface of my testicles. He knew right away that something wasn't right so he immediately ordered an ultra-sound examination at the hospital. He also gave me the name and number of an oncologist and for me to get in to see him immediately. I was stunned, numb but somehow focused at the task at hand. I had flashbacks in my mind from my previous experience with cancer, chemotherapy and the effects it had on me. I was in a flux.

I reached the hospital where I was shuttled around to the Ultra-sound department. I was a little shaken and acted like a scared grade-schooler being told of what to expect. My physician's diagnosis also proved correct as the technician told me that it does appear to be a mass in the area of concern. I took a deep breath and tried to put on a brave face. You hear about all different types of cancer and in the back of your mind, you never think you have to live that or face that possibility again. Here I am going through the same thing all over again. Well, let's get this done was my attitude. My anger was unmatched and nearly primal. I was pissed. Damn, damn, damn.

Upon meeting with this new oncologist, I am given the game plan on how we were going to attack this; surgery followed by 4 to 5 rounds of chemotherapy. Surgery was scheduled within a couple of weeks and the procedure was done as an outpatient procedure, so as long as I felt ok, I could go home the same day. I still could not believe I had testicular cancer.

Checking into the hospital, I still have an uneasy feeling and I am a little nervous. After getting settled in, they come for me and there is another wait in the surgical staging area. I meet with the anesthesiologist to go over what I could expect. Once I am finally brought in for my surgery, it seemed to be over in no time. I eventually come out of my fog and get sent back to my room. I am released a short while later and although I am feeling a little off, all I could think of was getting home and get some sleep. I was told that my surgery was successful and that the tumor was removed as well as my left testicle. In my mind, I am still functional and ok, shocked as hell, but ok. Tumor removed and hernia repaired.

I later meet with my new oncologist and his army of nurses who explained what else I could expect during chemotherapy. I began my treatment in December and it was scheduled to go until May or June of 2011, depending on how well I handled it. My oncologist decides to make sure my tumor has not spread to any other part of my body and orders a bone marrow test. This was one of the most painful procedures I would ever have while being awake. The procedure was done at his office. As I lay on my stomach, with my pants down, he inserted a needle to numb the eventual pain I would feel. Then, he inserts another needle that goes deep into my lower hip. I feel every bit of it and by now I am clenching my teeth and fists, trying to be as still as possible. He scrapes the surface of my hip bone and removes the needle. His nurse tries to comfort me, as she knows I am in complete agony. The sample is sent off for further testing, and luckily it comes back negative a few days later. No trace of cancer cells in my bone marrow. Thank God.

I later find out that my new oncologist has a new partner that was my late wife's oncologist. I know that name anywhere. I am shocked and surprised. Too loss for words, I never bring it up to her as I am face to face with this physician when she fills in for my physician later while I am in the hospital. Life is truly ironic.

My graduation is scheduled for June 2011. I am so excited, I could hardly contain myself. After all of those years of doubting myself, all those years of wondering if I had what it took to deliver, all came to an end. From January to May of 2011, I had undergone chemotherapy sessions all the while in school finishing up my last semester and cranking out papers for each class. It was tough. I had the physical look of a cancer patient; pale, loss of hair and a little weak. Despite this, I was not going to miss out on one of the biggest things I had achieved up to that point in my life. I made a conscious decision to not make any further arrangements to see my oncologist. I felt fine. He indicated that all I would need was the four or five treatments, which I had completed up to that point. I felt I was on my way to remission and on my way to finding a new career with the aid of having my bachelors' degree. Nothing was going to stop me. I was going to walk that stage and receive my diploma. I needed that affirmation after all I had gone through with employment over the years.

CHAPTER 6

No, Not Again

FALL 2011, I HAVE JUST started on my first semester of graduate school. I have not found the job I wanted, now that I have my degree but I am searching nonetheless. I started to have some constant pain in my lower back. I seem to be a bit tired lately. Once I see blood in my urine, I know something is terribly wrong. I am urinating straight blood. It was scary and eerie. I worked at a dialysis clinic at this time of my life. The nurses and my supervisor, who fancied herself as a medical specialist, have no real advice for me, just a look of concern and almost panic on their faces. Uh, oh. Here we go again. I go to the Emergency Room and have some tests run. It takes forever to see a physician as I am really concerned from what I am seeing. Again, I am told to see my primary physician with the specifics of condition. I already know what he will say and I choose to go back to the oncologist for follow up and the results of my emergency room tests. He knows and gives me the business about how I should have kept coming for treatments back in June. I remind him that he told me that all I needed was four to five treatments and I completed five before I made the decision to attend my commencement exercises that June. We have such a father-son relationship that it works for us.

It was at one of those later appointments at my oncologist's office when it was detected that I had a very quick pulse rate. It was in the

140+ beats per minute range. I never noticed anything different. I am ordered to get to the hospital and have an EKG exam. From there, it was determined that I had a blood clot and was put on blood thinners. Pulmonary Embolism, just like that, this was very serious as it could have had bad consequences for me. I am admitted into the hospital and have to stay about a week. I had no real pain or discomfort, just the thought of potential death stayed on my mind the entire time I was in the hospital.

Ultimately there was a rush for me to see a urologist to get on board with the team of doctors I was going to need. I was scheduled for surgery in January 2012 to remove a tumor in my mid-section. Due to the results of my blood test, it has shown that I have the hormonal level of a pregnant woman. There were to be a team of doctors available for my surgery due to the potential complications. This was going to be major surgery. My left kidney was removed during surgery as well as part of my bladder. All other traces of tumors were removed and I had a loss of six units of blood during the surgery. This surgery had me coming out far worse than I had in previous surgeries. My pain was excruciating. I was cold and miserable as I had to wait in recovery for a room to be made available. The nurses tried to keep me as comfortable as I could be, all things considering. I stayed in the hospital for about a week. I felt different, not quite myself. My sleeping arrangements were different at home. I had slept in a lounging chair in my bedroom. After a while that got old and I moved into my living room on a chair and ottoman. Nothing was really working for me but I made the most of it. I haven't slept in my bedroom, in my bed in over two years. My appetite was different and I went through soups, vegetable and fruit smoothies, Coco Wheats and Gatorade. That was all I could stand. This was very dark times for me. Getting comfortable and sleeping was going to be difficult as well in the ensuing weeks.

After a while, I noticed that my bowel movements were different. I had stool in my urine and my bowel movements were watery. Very weird. Once I had a follow up with my doctor, surgery was going to be needed again to fix this new issue. I was given a nephrostomy tube and bag that runs from my only surviving kidney and a colostomy bag that essentially routes my bowels to a bag that hangs off the front of my stomach. Great. Having the urge to not use the bathroom is weird and very unnatural.

I had to learn how to monitor and drain these bags for the time being as theses were temporary solutions for my problem of cancer. I had a re-routing surgery done and it changed everything.

Two surgeries within a couple of months were a bit much for my body. I felt beat up and tired, but I pressed on. In my mind I always felt I was going to be ok, I just needed a couple of months and I'd bounce back. Not so. Walking around my living room and kitchen with a walker was now going to be my physical therapy. Each passing day seem to wear me out to the point that I would purposely not get up from my chair, due to pure exhaustion and constant pain. I was taking pain medication like Tic-Tacs. My wife would fuss at me to get up and walk as if nothing was wrong with me and I would look at her with a look of disgust and disdain. "Are you fucking serious? I am doing the best I can! Leave me alone! I am tired!" It got so bad that I could not move my legs one night. I could not stand up. I stared at my legs begging them to move. Nothing. She called the paramedics at my request because I knew something was really wrong. They placed me in a wheel chair and whisked me off to the Emergency Room where I was told that I had an infection. I was admitted into the hospital again. While I was given antibiotics for Sepsis, my oncologist ordered me to undergo chemo sessions while I was there. At that point, we'd agree that I would carry on and not have any further interruptions with my treatments.

My initial session went ok, as I was extremely fatigued on the third day. From that point on, I was gone. In May of 2012, I had slipped into a "Neurotoxicity" that essentially put me into a mini-coma. I was in a deep sleep for about two weeks, I was told. I had wires clamped on my head, tubes placed in my mouth and my heart monitored. My team of doctors were all perplexed. I had a heart specialist, nephrologists, neurologist, oncologist, my primary physician and an infectious disease specialist. No one except for the oncologist, had any idea if I'd ever come out of it. He knew that the chemotherapy was too heavy of a dose and that it would take some time to get out of my body. There were practically last rites given for me at the hospital, but my wife and parents listened to the oncologist and stayed prayerful at my bedside. They took turns to wait on me for two weeks. In their hearts, they felt that I would make it and awaken. It's not every day that a patient reaches this stage. I became an oddity of sorts at the hospital. Even in near death, gossip follows me.

For me, I felt trapped in a dream I could not wake up from. It was like being in a maze, filled with characters and people who came to my bedside. It all took place in a hospital, in the Maternity Ward. I heard a constant, loud noise in my head. It was always cold. For you see, if anyone came near me and spoke around my sleeping body, they became a part of my dream. My eyes were always open. It became so illogical yet so clear and concise. Think of "Alice in Wonderland," written by Stephen King, with an element of evil vs. good thrown in. I saw light. I was given choices to go with the false idol (preacher) or go back with my mother, who made a better pot of coffee. Weird, huh?

Once I began to wake up, my mind was like a computer needing to be rebooted. All of my memories were foggy and unclear. I could not stop talking. I was really freaking my wife out. I was talking fast and illogical. What seemed like reality in my dreams was not a reality in this life. I had dreamed that my wife and I had another child. It felt so real that I believed it to be true for weeks after I awoke. I had to learn what was real and what a part of my dream was. It was surreal. I had to learn how to eat and drink. Ice chips and applesauce would be my main source of nutrients. I had lost about one hundred pounds from my initial surgery in January to the present day in June. I felt weak and feeble.

Once I showed signs of physical healing, the plan was for me to be admitted into a rehabilitation facility. This would aid me in getting nutrients into my body through IV since eating had become so burdensome for me. I was very weak. I had no idea how bad I looked. I had to learn how to walk again. Being in that facility made me realize how lucky I was, as well as how much work I was going to need. I was pretty miserable. I wanted to get out as soon as possible. Hours became days, days became weeks. I tried to make the most of it by making new friends at this place. My nurses and physical therapists became the closest thing I had to family, for the location of this place was about 40 minutes from my home. Even though I had my own room, it was cold all the time and too quiet for any real comfort. Some of the technicians are strange and odd. My hands stay cold all the time. All I could think about was showing signs of being well, so that I could go home. My first born's (daughter) prom and graduation was coming up and I just had to be there! Every parent thinks about those days. Those are major milestones in any child's life. Being there and being a part of the process as a parent lasts forever.

CHAPTER 7

Road to Recovery

*I*T WAS NOT TO BE. I was going to have to settle for seeing pictures of her prom and a visit from her with her cap and gown on after graduation. I cried my eyes out for days. I was supposed to be there. I was supposed to be there. How could this happen again? First her mom and now me? I was so angry and hurt. It wasn't how I planned for all of these years! Luckily, my wife stepped up and took over all of the planning of my daughter's special days along with her sister. Prom essentials were taken care of, graduation essentials were taken care of, graduation party was taken care of, all I had to do was get well and get out of there as soon as I could.

Remarkably, my daughter handled this difficult time with grace and resolve. Her mind may have been on me and my eventual recovery but she managed to have a good time, which was very important to me. She and my son may have been victims of having both parents obtain cancer, but that should not be their only memory in their life. That was important to me. They need to have good memories of their childhood. There was some solace in that my wife took control of everything in our lives. She had to become me, in order to keep things moving along. It's a huge burden. She had to make all decisions on every topic within our life and the children's life. I have lived it before, so now I hope she truly knows how I felt for all of those years leading up to when we met. The only difference is that I am still here. Not everyone can truly handle that kind of load. I give her a lot of credit.

While I was shuttled around from the hospital and to the rehabilitation facility, my former mother-in-law had taken seriously ill and later passed away. It was very difficult for me to accept it. She was one of the warmest and funniest people I ever knew. She and I were so close that after Debbie passed away, we talked on the phone at least twice a month, keeping the tradition she had with her daughter. She entrusted me to take care of her baby, and I took that to heart until she passed away. I made it a point to see her and make a trip down south to Mississippi after Debbie's death. After all, she still saw me as her son. I was definitely going to miss her. Not being able to say goodbye made me numb for a few days after hearing of her death. I wanted to be there for her services out of state in the worst way, but it was not to be. I had so much going on physically, that I had no real choice but to try to get better.

Another death in the family came to my uncle on my biological father's side. He was the patriarch of the family and lived 10 minutes away from my home. A widower himself, he and I shared some other similarities as well; three kids (2 girls and a boy), unknowingly lived in the same community at one point of our lives and sounded alike over the phone. We also shared the same urologist, as we bumped into each other at an appointment and we both had cancer. I really looked up to him and found him to be warm, friendly, very sensible and practical, a real great man to know. As I was recovering at home from surgery, I could not attend his funeral services as well. That was pretty painful and sad for me. It was beginning to be a load I could hardly bear. Despair would constantly be on my mind for weeks. My wife attended the services, filling in for me. He and I were supposed to get together for lunch, but.

I am sent back to the hospital for chemotherapy which meant that I'd be there for about two weeks until I am sent back to the rehabilitation facility again. This would go on for another three times. Back and forth, back and forth the ambulance would whisk me away into the night. I manage to catch some warm breeze on my cold body with each trip. It was the hottest temperatures in recent memory and I could not enjoy it with my freezing body. It was those little things that gave me comfort in my misery. With each trip, I practically begged the paramedics to walk slowly so I could enjoy the moment. I was cooped up in a hospital and needed some fresh air.

As a patient at the rehabilitation facility, I befriend the Chaplain and Medical Director. It was with my chance meeting with the director that I realized that he was the son of a man I worked with at the federal court. His father was an executive at the courts. The Medical Director was a junior as his name tag gave him away. His father and I had been teammates on the softball team I managed and played pickup basketball games at lunch time. We were so close, that he and his wife attended my wedding to Debbie in 1995. Wow. Talk about a small world. That made all of the difference as the son made sure to see me every day and give me updates on my condition.

It was also during this time that my conversations with the Chaplain would be therapeutic for me. I bared my soul to this kind woman who asked all the right questions that made me open up and realize that I had purpose in this life. For that, I am eternally grateful that the good Lord sent her to my life. With each trip back to the hospital I am met with open arms as it seemed like I was familiar with every staff member on every floor. "Mr. Lavizzo, you're back! You look better! You look good! Good to see you again!" I heard those kind words every time. Those meant the world to me. My medical history became such fodder, it was like being an employee of the hospital. My whole life was like an open book to these people. They knew everything about me. I spent way too much time in the hospital and rehabilitation facility.

I have had many surgical procedures, having ports placed, removed and replaced back in my body. It is handled like an outpatient procedure but it gets old after a while. I am not a fan of getting stuck time after time. I don't like it at all. I hate needles. It is something that I will have to endure throughout this time. I still have much to fix and repair in my body in the coming years.

CHAPTER 8

Home Sweet Home

I AM FINALLY SENT HOME SEPTEMBER of 2013. I could hardly believe it. All I could think about was being in my home and getting better. To leave the hospital was a major milestone. I had been away from my home for a year and a half, nearly dying in the process. I recognized the moment and tried to see the larger picture. This was still going to take some time, getting better, but I was up for it. I had no other choice. I was also informed that because of the chemotherapy, I started to show signs that my remaining kidney was failing. My creatine level was increasing. Dialysis was going to be needed. Damn. I felt like I was getting close to complete recovery only to be told that I would have to undergo dialysis three days a week. I am also assigned a home health nurse, who comes by once a week to check my vitals, medication list and change my remaining wound dressings. She came at a time when I was not in the mood to be touched or prodded, but I endure it nonetheless. I grow on her after a while. I like her. She becomes my surrogate wife as we talk about everything; children, life, work, health, and other family members. She takes good care of me. I completely trust her. God sent her to help take care of me, for this I am sure.

Working at a dialysis clinic for two years prior to my illness allowed me to see patients in an entirely new light. I was their cheerleader, their confidant, their business handler. My position was titled Administrative

Assistant to the Unit Manager, but my duties were all encompassing. I did it all. I witnessed things there that an everyday person could not handle. Death in the chair (coding), contacting family members and making them aware of their loved one's condition was a daunting task. I learned a lot. I stayed cool under pressure to contact paramedics and getting the important information they would need upon arrival to the clinic. I handled many duties and was very flexible and professional.

Now, I am one of them. I became the patient. How long was this to be? No one knows for sure. What I am sure of is that there is a chance I still could completely recover and no longer need dialysis. We'll see.

While recovering at home, I began to feel ill. I was throwing up and nothing was passing through to my colostomy bag. I waited a couple of days before I checked myself into the hospital. I was not up for another "visit" as I was sick to the idea of coming here. There have been so many procedures done, so many sticks to my skin looking for blood, so many hours wasted in the Emergency Room. I was smart enough to call my oncologist and my nephrologists, as so they could get me into the hospital quickly. Since I was a "frequent flyer" of sorts, I was able to get checked in where they ran several tests. I had a blockage in my abdomen which kept me from passing any food. I was pretty miserable for a few days. Surgery was an option but my surgeon who previously performed all of my previous surgeries prescribed a shot which would cause me sweatiness, nausea, dizziness and an uncontrollable feeling of pain. It would last for about 15 minutes. It was like a train ran through my head. I was cured! I was having bowel movements again and was released in a few days. Thank God for no surgeries!

It's now 2014, on the cusp of complete remission from testicular cancer, I can't help but think about my long road to recovery. I often find myself thinking about my past experiences and how hard getting through this disease was for me. Sometimes while in deep thought, I cry my eyes out. Not being in any physical pain, but the emotional toll and how it has affected me and my wife. The thought of being in a mini-coma is very unsettling. The thought of my parents, wife, children and family standing over me in a condition I had no control over haunts me. No one should want to be seen that way. I think of that all of the time. The toll my psyche has taken has been brutal. Am I any better than I was before I was afflicted with this cancer? In some sense, I'd like to think that I will be. I will need to make drastic changes in my life in order to be able to completely move on.

Physically, I am not so sure my body will ever be the same. I am not as limber any more. I am noticeably different physically as any person would who loses 100+ pounds. I hope that this form of cancer will not come back. I don't think I can endure this nightmare again. I am beat up, mentally and physically. I still have many things to accomplish in my life. I have to walk my girls down the isle at their future weddings. I want to be a grandfather. I would like to obtain my masters' degree in Public Administration. Hearing my girls laugh while they watch television, taking calls from my son while he is in another state, those are the little things I fought to stay here. It's comforting to me and makes me realize why I am still here. A hero is still needed, a hero to them. I still have softball games to attend, recitals to take in, graduations to reflect on. With all of my might, I need to be there. I will be there.

Yet, I am also reminded that all of my health issues have taken a toll on my wife. Our relationship is crumbling before my eyes. I realize it and I am very contrite about it. There is nothing I can do about it as I will not give in trying to be a hero where I am not needed. I am still overwhelmed by having to get better physically. That is where I am needed, to be there for myself. If you cannot understand that, then to hell with you. After all of these years, it is time for me to look out for me. I owe that to myself. I still have harder battles to win.

The many rounds of chemotherapy have left me with a condition called Peripheral Neuropathy, which means nerve damage. I have numbness, pain, loss of sensation in my feet and hands. My hands are always cold and stiff. Typing has now become a challenge as I cannot fully feel where my fingers are in tuned to the keyboard. My balance is a little off due to not having sensation in my feet. I may never fully regain that normal feeling in those areas because nerve damage seems to be one of those physical ailments that have no real clear-cut cure. I take pain medication to ease the pain but it is never totally gone. The emotional toll will always be with me. I often have thoughts of how things used to be, but that will always be a chapter of my life that will have to remain in the past. "Look towards the future" should be my motto, but I keep peeking over my shoulder of my past. No constant aches and pains, no constant doctor's appointments, no routine nurse's visits at home, no worries about the next new revelation about my body, these are all pressing issues for me. In my mind, I want to be rid of it all. Everything.

Pressing forward, I realize that I have been given another chance at life. Another chance at maybe correcting the mistakes I've made before, another chance to live my life another way keeps me focused. I am contrite. I am repentant and very humbled. I have a short tolerance for bull shit and nonsense. I want to share a part of me that I may have unwittingly kept away from those I truly love all of those years. Is that even possible? I believe so. Is it too late? I hope not. Is that my purpose? I hope so. I am eternally grateful for all of the doctors, nurses, medical professionals and my family for aiding me in getting my life back on track. Those are the heroes who need to be mentioned. I would not be here if it weren't for them.

I ache for the chance of seeing old friends, old classmates, and old neighbors. I miss them all so much. They represent my past, they aided me in making me who I am today. I yearn for the laughter, the companionship we once shared. It is who I am, who I yearn to be again. For this much is true, we are not guaranteed an extended life on this earth. I want to make the most of my time while I am still here. I have endured much and will continue to do so. Managing stress and relationships will be the key as I feel that I have much work yet to do and to learn. Isn't that the point of living? The very essence of surviving and living depends on one's ability to endure and to keep learning.

Acknowledgements

*T*HIS BOOK IS DEDICATED TO *my parents, Richard and Goldie Lavizzo, who sacrificed much to ensure my safety, my education and my well being. Those are things that should never be overlooked. I am who I am based on their beliefs and ever-lasting love. I can only hope to be half the parent to my children as you were to me. Love you so much y'all! I'd like to thank my father, Clifton Hill, for creating me, giving me all of the traits I would need to make it in this world. I would like to thank my children; Michael Alexander, Taylor Marie and Kira Pearl, you all have made me the parent I'd always hope to be. I may have made and molded you, but you in turn have made me a better person and a better man. I'd be remiss if I also did not acknowledge my wife, Tracy. You have always been the strong, purposeful woman I know you could be. You are my strength, my guide, my spouse in every sense of the word. May you find your purpose, and shall you embrace it fully. To Professor Marilyn Yirku of Governors State University, thank you for helping me find my voice. You were the driving force for this book and it would not be if it weren't for you. To my family, my brothers, David and Steven, you aided me in my direst hours, in my darkest depths. You were some of the most influential siblings a person could ever have. Thank you so much for being my big brothers. To my older sisters, Sheilah, Susan and Laura, thank you for your constant watch and prayers over me. Thank you for being great role-models in our family. Stay blessed. To my extended family, the Hills and the Lavizzo's, my uncles, aunts, cousins, nephews and nieces, to know that I was on your mind during my dire circumstances is so comforting. Words cannot express how much I love you and how much you mean to this family. To all of my in-laws, thank you for being there for my family, it meant so much to me. To my physicians, nurses, technicians and medical staff of Advocate South Suburban and RML Rehabilitation, thank you so much for looking over me, taking care of me and helping me get through this disease. I couldn't have done it without you. To all of my friends, former co-workers, thank you for your visits, phone calls and visits over the years. Thank you for the much needed laughter, it was my beacon of hope. Thank you to all of my relatives who preceded me in death. You are the inspiration for this book. You have shaped me and touched my life in so many ways. And finally to my other brothers, my old classmates, teammates, the B.O.Y.Z.'s, you all are my constant reminder of what is good in this life, thank you for being who you are. We are brothers for life and I love you!*